the low fat asian book

charmaine solomon

HAMLYN

First published in Great Britain in 1999 by Hamlyn
an imprint of Reed Consumer Books Limited
Michelin House, 81 Fulham Road
London SW3 6RB
and Auckland and Melbourne

Produced and published in Australia by
New Holland Publishers (Australia) Pty Ltd
Sydney • London • Cape Town

14 Aquatic Drive, Frenchs Forest, NSW 2086,
Australia

24 Nutford Place, London WIH 6DQ
United Kingdom

80 McKenzie Street, Cape Town 8001
South Africa

ISBN 0 600 59730 X

Publishing General Manager: Jane Hazell
Publishers: Clare Coney, Averill Chase
Designer: Guy Mirabella
Design Assistant: Laurence Lemmon-Warde
Styling: Margaret Alcock
Food cooked by: Nina Harris, Jill Pavey
China: Villeroy & Boch, Australia Pty Ltd
Quark Xpress: Melbourne Media Services
Printer: L Rex Printing, China

contents

combination long soup

One of those soups which can be an entire meal. As a meal it will make 3 servings rather than 6.

serves 6

6 dried shiitake mushrooms
2 eggs, beaten
 salt and pepper to taste
 few drops sesame oil
250 g (8 oz) fine egg noodles
8 cups chicken stock (see page 91)
3 teaspoons peanut oil
1 clove garlic, peeled and bruised

2 slices fresh ginger
250 g (8 oz) lean pork or chicken, finely shredded
3 cups white Chinese cabbage, cut in strips
1 piece canned winter bamboo shoot, diced
2 tablespoons light soy sauce
1 tablespoon dry sherry
½ teaspoon sesame oil

Soak the mushrooms in hot water for 30 minutes. Remove and discard the stems and slice the caps finely. Season the eggs with a little salt and pepper. Lightly grease a heated omelette pan with a few drops of sesame oil. Pour in enough beaten egg to make a thin omelette. Repeat with remaining egg. Slice omelettes finely and set aside.

Cook noodles for 2 minutes in a large pot of boiling water. (If the noodles are in tight bundles, soak in warm water first for 10 minutes to separate strands and ensure even cooking. Lift out on a slotted spoon and drop into boiling water.) Drain in a colander and rinse with cold water to separate. Drain again. Heat the chicken stock.

Meanwhile heat the peanut oil in a wok; stir-fry the garlic and ginger, discarding when brown. Add the pork or chicken to wok and fry quickly, stirring, until the colour changes. Add the cabbage and the bamboo shoot and stir-fry 2 minutes more.

Add noodles and fried mixture to chicken stock. Return to boil. Add soy sauce, sherry and salt to taste. Stir in sesame oil and serve immediately, garnished with the omelette strips.

mixed meat and vegetable soup

serves 6

- 4 dried shiitake mushrooms
- 125 g (4 oz) chicken fillets
- 2 stalks Chinese broccoli (gai larn)
- 125 g (4 oz) lean barbecued pork or roast pork, diced
- 1 tablespoon peanut oil
- ½ teaspoon finely grated ginger
- ½ teaspoon crushed garlic
- 6 cups chicken stock (see page 91)
- 2 tablespoons dry sherry
- 2 tablespoons oyster sauce
- 2 tablespoons cornflour

Soak the mushrooms in hot water for 30 minutes. Discard the stems and slice the caps thinly. Cut the chicken into paper-thin slices, partially freezing meat first. Cut the broccoli stems diagonally into thin slices.

Heat half the oil in a wok, add ginger and garlic and stir for a few seconds, then add broccoli and toss over high heat until colour deepens. Remove to dish. Heat the remaining oil and stir-fry the chicken.

Bring the chicken stock to the boil. Add the sherry, oyster sauce, chicken, broccoli, sliced mushrooms and pork. Mix the cornflour with ¼ cup cold water and add to the soup, stirring constantly, until soup is thickened and clear. Serve immediately.

short soup

This soup is so named because of its 'short' dumplings or wontons.

serves 6

3 dried shiitake mushrooms
125 g (4 oz) raw prawns
125 g (4 oz) minced pork
salt to taste
1 tablespoon light soy sauce
1 small clove garlic, crushed
¼ teaspoon finely grated fresh ginger
4 spring onions, finely chopped
125 g (4 oz) wonton wrappers
2 litres (8 cups) chicken stock (see page 91)
½ teaspoon oriental sesame oil

Soak mushrooms in hot water for 30 minutes. Squeeze dry, discard the stems and finely chop the caps. Shell and devein the prawns. Chop finely. Combine the mushrooms with the prawns, pork, salt, soy sauce, garlic, ginger and half the spring onions.

Put a level teaspoon of mixture in centre of each wonton wrapper, moisten the edges with water and fold diagonally to form a triangle. Press edges to seal. Moisten 2 corners at the base of the triangle and join. Drop wontons into boiling stock and stir until it boils again. Simmer for 10 minutes. Sprinkle with sesame oil and remaining spring onions.

chicken
and bean curd sour soup

serves 6

185 g (6 oz) cooked chicken (skin and bones removed)
185 g (6 oz) firm bean curd
6 dried shiitake mushrooms
185 g (6 oz) bamboo shoot, or celery stalk
90 g (3 oz) snow peas
6 cups chicken stock (see page 91)

3 tablespoons rice vinegar or white wine vinegar
1 teaspoon freshly ground black pepper
1½ tablespoons light soy sauce
1 large egg, lightly beaten

Dice chicken and bean curd. Soak mushrooms in hot water for 30 minutes, remove stems and discard. Slice caps into thin strips. Cut the bamboo shoot or celery stalk into julienne strips. Remove strings from snow peas and slice diagonally into 2 or 3 pieces. Bring the stock to boil and add the chicken, bean curd, mushrooms and bamboo shoot or celery and simmer for 3 or 4 minutes. Add the snow peas, vinegar and pepper and simmer for 1 minute more. Whisk the soy sauce into the beaten egg. Increase the heat under the pan and pour in the beaten egg and soy sauce in a steady stream. Serve immediately.

prawn ball soup

serves 6

500 g (1 lb) raw prawns, shelled and deveined
½ teaspoon finely grated fresh ginger
2 slices soft white bread, crumbed
cornflour
1 teaspoon salt
6 cups prawn or chicken stock
¼ teaspoon oriental sesame oil
2 tablespoons finely chopped spring onions

Chop prawns finely. Mix with ginger, breadcrumbs, 2 teaspoons cornflour and salt. Make the mixture into balls, then simmer in the stock. Thicken with 1 tablespoon cornflour. Add the sesame oil and the spring onions. Serve immediately.

soup with vegetables

serves 4

6 cups chicken stock
24 small sprigs broccoli
120 g (4 oz) snow peas or sugar snap peas
4 tablespoons finely chopped coriander leaves
few drops sesame oil

Bring the chicken stock to boil. Add the broccoli and cook for about 4 minutes. Add the peas and cook for 2 minutes more. Remove from heat. Stir in coriander and sesame oil and serve immediately.

chicken velvet soup

The velvety texture created by the very finely chopped chicken breast gives this soup its name.

serves 6

500 g (1 lb) chicken breast fillets
½ teaspoon salt
3 egg whites
7 cups chicken stock (see page 91)
375 g (12 oz) canned creamed corn
2 tablespoons cornflour
½ teaspoon sesame oil
1 tablespoon dry sherry
2 thin slices lean smoked ham, finely chopped

Chop the chicken very finely until almost puréed or use a food processor. Add salt and 3 tablespoons cold water; mix well. Beat egg whites until frothy and fold into chicken purée. Reserve.

In a saucepan, bring chicken stock to boil; stir in corn. Mix cornflour with ¼ cup cold water. Bring stock mixture back to boil and stir in cornflour. Return to boil, stirring until thickened. Stir in sesame oil, sherry and reserved chicken. Simmer, stirring, for 2 or 3 minutes. Serve immediately sprinkled with ham.

Thai
soup with stuffed mushrooms

serves 4

- 12 medium dried shiitake mushrooms
- 2 spring onions, including some green
- 120 g (4 oz) minced pork or chopped raw prawns
- 1 teaspoon finely chopped garlic
- 4 teaspoons finely chopped coriander leaves

- 4 teaspoons Maggi Seasoning ground black pepper to taste
- 4 teaspoons finely chopped water chestnuts
- 6 cups chicken stock, fat removed
- ½ medium green cucumber
- 4 teaspoons fish sauce, or to taste

Pour very hot water over mushrooms in a bowl and leave to soak for 30 minutes. Drain, squeeze out excess water; cut off and discard stems. Cut several diagonal slices from spring onion and set aside, covered. Finely chop remainder. Combine pork or prawns with garlic, finely chopped spring onion, coriander, Maggi Seasoning, pepper and water chestnuts. Mix well. Pack mixture into drained mushroom caps and cook for about 15 minutes in 3 cups of stock. (It is important to cook in only a small amount of stock so that the filling remains intact in the mushrooms until cooked.) Peel cucumber; cut in halves lengthwise, scoop out seeds and cut cucumber across into thin slices.

Add remaining stock, fish sauce and cucumber slices to saucepan and simmer for 3 or 4 minutes. Place 3 mushrooms in each soup plate and ladle soup over mushrooms. Garnish with reserved spring onion slices.

egg flower soup

This Chinese soup takes its name from the fact that the beaten egg looks like chrysanthemum petals when poured into boiling stock.

serves 4

6 cups chicken stock
2 tablespoons dry sherry
½ teaspoon sesame oil
   salt to taste
2 eggs, beaten
2 spring onions finely sliced

Bring stock to boil. Add sherry, sesame oil, and salt if necessary. Slowly pour beaten egg into boiling stock. Stir once or twice. Serve immediately, sprinkled with spring onion.

green beans with prawns

serves 6

625 g (1¼ lb) small raw prawns
625 g (1¼ lb) green beans
1 tablespoon vegetable oil
½ tablespoon sesame oil
1 large onion, sliced thinly
4 tablespoons light soy sauce
1½ teaspoons sugar
1 tablespoon toasted, crushed
   sesame seeds

Shell and devein the prawns and chop roughly. Trim the beans and remove strings if necessary. Cut into thin diagonal slices. Heat oils in wok and stir-fry the onion and prawns for 2 minutes; add the beans and stir-fry for another 3 minutes. Add the remaining ingredients, mixing well. Cover and simmer over low heat until the beans are just tender—about 6 to 8 minutes. Do not overcook. Serve immediately.

braised fish and prawn rolls

serves 4

16 raw prawns
750 g (1½ lb) firm white fish fillets
2 tablespoons peanut oil
6 thin slices fresh ginger
2 tablespoons light soy sauce
2 tablespoons dry sherry
4 spring onions, sliced finely

Shell and devein the prawns. Remove the skin and any bones from the fish fillets and cut them into 8 strips, each large enough to roll round a prawn. Fasten with wooden toothpicks. Heat the oil in a wok; add slices of ginger and fry until golden. Add fish rolls and fry for 2 minutes, turning carefully with tongs.

Drain excess oil from wok. Add ¼ cup hot water with soy sauce and sherry. Cover and simmer for 2 minutes or until fish is opaque. Transfer fish rolls to serving dish. Discard slices of ginger and remove toothpicks. Add spring onions to wok and stir until bright green. Pour sauce over fish.

Szechwan -style steamed fish

serves 4

2 whole fish, about 1.5 kg (3 lb)
1 teaspoon salt
1 teaspoon finely grated fresh
    ginger
2 tablespoons dry sherry
1 tablespoon peanut oil
1 teaspoon sesame oil
2 teaspoons crushed garlic
2 teaspoons finely chopped fresh
    ginger
4 teaspoons chilli bean sauce
4 spring onions, finely sliced
4 tablespoons chopped fresh
    coriander leaves

Purchase the fish cleaned and scaled. Slash diagonally. Rub over with salt and grated ginger. Place in a lightly oiled heatproof dish and steam over boiling water for 8 to 10 minutes. Pour off liquid that collects around fish into a measuring cup. Add sherry. Heat peanut and sesame oils in a wok or heavy pan. Add garlic and ginger and stir-fry for 1 minute. Add bean sauce, sherry mixture and spring onions; bring to boil. Pour over fish and garnish with coriander. Serve with rice.

grilled fish on skewers

serves 6

1 kg (2 lb) snapper, gemfish or similar thick white fillets with skin
2 teaspoons finely grated fresh ginger
3 cloves garlic, crushed
salt to taste
1 tablespoon ground coriander
1 teaspoon garam masala (see page 91)
½ teaspoon chilli powder
¼ teaspoon turmeric
¼ cup lime juice
1 cup plain yoghurt
2 tablespoons plain flour

Wash the fish and dry on paper towels, then cut into 5 cm (2 in) pieces. Thoroughly mix remaining ingredients in a bowl. Add fish pieces and fold gently until each piece is coated in marinade. Let stand for 15 minutes. Thread pieces of fish onto skewers — about 5 on each — making sure that skin is on one side. Put skewers on preheated grill and cook about 10 cm (4 in) away from heat. Make sure that skin is towards heat. Grill for 4 minutes, then turn skewers and grill other side for a further 4 minutes. Do not overcook. Fish will turn opaque when ready. Serve immediately accompanied by rice and salad or fresh chutneys.

ocean perch with bean sauce

serves 4

500 g (1 lb) ocean perch fillets
1 teaspoon finely grated fresh ginger
salt to taste
1 tablespoon brown bean sauce
1 tablespoon dry sherry
1 tablespoon peanut oil
2 thin slices ginger, shredded finely
3 spring onions, shredded finely
2 cloves garlic, chopped finely

Rub fillets with grated ginger and salt and put in a heatproof dish. Cover and steam for about 5 minutes or until done. Add the liquid that collects in dish to bean sauce and sherry.

Heat the oil and fry ginger, spring onions and garlic for 1 minute. Stir in sauce mixture and spoon over fish.

steamed fish with mushroom sauce

serves 4

- 4 dried shiitake mushrooms
- 500 g (1 lb) snapper, bream or similar white fish fillets
- salt and pepper to taste
- 1 teaspoon finely grated fresh ginger
- sesame oil
- ½ tablespoon peanut oil
- 4 spring onions, chopped
- 1 clove garlic, chopped finely
- 1 tablespoon soy sauce
- 1 cup stock (fish or chicken)
- 1 teaspoon cornflour
- fresh coriander leaves

Soak mushrooms in hot water for 30 minutes. Discard the stems and cut the caps into fine slices. Remove skin from fish fillets, season with salt and pepper and rub surface with ginger. Put on a plate lightly greased with sesame oil and sprinkle a little more sesame oil on top. Set aside.

Heat the peanut oil in a wok and fry the spring onions and garlic for a few seconds. Add the mushrooms, soy sauce, and stock and simmer for 10 minutes. Mix the cornflour with 1 tablespoon of cold water and add it to the wok. Stir until the sauce clears and thickens.

Keep the sauce warm while steaming the fish. Place the plate with the fillets in a steamer over boiling water for about 5 minutes or until flesh becomes opaque and flakes easily.

Carefully transfer fish to serving dish. Pour the sauce over it and sprinkle with coriander leaves to serve.

abalone
with vinegar and sesame

A Japanese dish served in small, deep bowls as an appetiser or side salad.

serves 6–8

1 can Japanese abalone
2 small seedless green cucumbers
   salt to taste

Dressing
2 tablespoons sesame seeds
½ teaspoon finely grated fresh
   ginger
1 tablespoon sugar
¼ cup rice vinegar or mild white
   wine vinegar
1 sheet nori (dried seaweed)

Drain abalone and cut into paper-thin slices. Cut cucumbers in halves lengthwise. Cut across into thin slices. Place in a colander, sprinkling with a little salt and leave to drain for 20 minutes. Rinse briefly with cold water. Lean to drain well.

Dressing: Toast sesame seeds in a dry pan over medium heat, stirring constantly, until golden—this should only take a few minutes. Turn out to cool, then crush slightly with a mortar and pestle or in a blender. Mix with ginger, sugar, vinegar and 2 tablespoons water. Lightly toast nori until crisp, and cut into thin strips with kitchen scissors.

Mix abalone and cucumber slices; pour dressing over and chill. Serve sprinkled with shredded nori.

fish
in chilli tomato sauce

Since this is an acid-based curry, it is best to cook it in a non-aluminium pan.

serves 4

750 g (1½ lb) fish fillets
3 tablespoons vinegar
3 tablespoons fish sauce
2 tablespoons hot chilli sauce
3 teaspoons brown sugar
½ tablespoon oil
3 onions, chopped finely
500 g (1 lb) ripe tomatoes, peeled,
    seeded and chopped
1 sprig fresh coriander leaves
2 or 3 red chillies, finely sliced
    and seeded

Rinse the fish and dry on paper towels. In a small bowl mix vinegar, fish sauce, chilli sauce and brown sugar, stirring to dissolve sugar.

Heat the oil in a heavy based pan and fry the onions over low heat, stirring frequently, until soft and beginning to turn golden. Add tomatoes and vinegar mixture, cover and simmer for 15 to 20 minutes until sauce is thick. Add fish fillets, spooning sauce over them. Cover and cook gently until fish is done. Do not overcook. Serve garnished with coriander leaves and sliced red chillies.

grilled mixed seafood

1 small clove garlic
1 teaspoon sugar
½ teaspoon finely grated fresh
   ginger
3 tablespoons Japanese soy
   sauce
4 small ling or snapper fillets or
   steaks
8 large raw prawns
8 fresh oysters
8 fresh scallops
1 large green capsicum
1 small eggplant
   vegetable oil for cooking

Dipping sauce
½ cup Japanese soy sauce
¼ cup rice wine (mirin)
3 teaspoons sugar
1 teaspoon finely grated fresh
   ginger
½ teaspoon oriental sesame oil

Crush garlic with sugar and mix with ginger and soy sauce in a bowl. Add the fish fillets, turning until they are coated in marinade. Set aside for 30 minutes. Meanwhile shell and devein prawns, leaving the tail intact. Drain any liquid from the oysters. Remove any dark streaks from the scallops, rinse briefly and drain. Cut the capsicum lengthwise into eights, discarding seeds and membranes. Slice the eggplant across into rounds.

Heat barbecue hotplate or griddle and grease lightly. Start with capsicum and eggplant as they take longer to cook, then add fish fillets, prawns, oysters and scallops as required and cook just until done. Turn pieces over to ensure even cooking and be careful not to overcook as this will make the seafood dry and tough. Oysters and scallops need a very short cooking time — just enough to heat them through. Serve with Dipping Sauce and hot white rice.

Dipping sauce: Mix soy sauce, rice wine, sugar, ginger and sesame oil, stirring until sugar is dissolved. Divide among individual sauce bowls.

steamed egg custard with seafood

In Japan this custard is regarded as a soup and eaten with a spoon. In summer the dish may be served cold.

serves 6

- 6 dried shiitake mushrooms
- 3 tablespoons Japanese soy sauce
- 1½ tablespoons sugar
- 6 small prawns
- 6 fresh oysters or scallops

- 6 eggs
- 3½ cups dashi stock (see note)
- 1½ teaspoons salt or to taste
- 3 tablespoons sake, mirin or dry sherry

Soak mushrooms in hot water for 30 minutes. Cut off stems and discard. Simmer the caps in a small saucepan with 1 cup soaking water, 1½ tablespoons of the soy sauce and the sugar for 8 to 10 minutes. Shell and devein the prawns. Meanwhile, prepare custard. Beat eggs, then stir in all other ingredients, plus remaining 1½ tablespoons soy sauce.

In individual custard cups or ramekins (or use chawan mushi cups if you have them) place a mushroom, a prawn, and an oyster or scallop. Fill cups with the custard mixture, carefully skimming any bubbles from the top of the mixture. Place cups in a baking pan with hot water to come halfway up the sides. Bake in moderate oven for 15 minutes or until set. Serve hot or cold.

Note: Make up dashi stock following instructions on packet or bottle of dashi concentrate.

steamed scallops with ginger wine

serves 6

- 18 scallops on the half shell
- 1 teaspoon finely grated fresh ginger
- 2 teaspoons oyster sauce
- 3 tablespoons green ginger wine
- 1 teaspoon sugar

Remove vein from scallops but leave roe attached. Combine all remaining ingredients and stir to dissolve sugar. Add scallops to mixture, cover and refrigerate for at least 30 minutes.

Put one scallop (or two if shells are large) on each shell and place on a wire rack in a bamboo steamer. Cover and steam over boiling water for 5 minutes. Serve immediately with rice.

simmered
seafood and vegetables

A Japanese dish served in soup bowls with a dipping sauce. You can substitute other varieties of seafood or vegetables. Make dipping sauce ahead of time and cool.

serves 4–6

500 g (1 lb) snapper or bream fillets
1 lobster tail
1 cup cooked and drained bean thread vermicelli
8 cups dashi (use dried or liquid instant dashi and follow instructions on label)
2 small carrots, sliced
small piece kombu (Japanese dried kelp)
soy sauce to taste

100 g (3½ oz) fresh mushrooms, sliced
6 spring onions, cut into bite-size lengths

Dipping sauce
1 cup dashi
¼ cup Japanese soy sauce
¼ cup mirin or dry sherry
pinch salt or sugar

Wash the fish and cut into 2.5 cm (1 in) pieces. With a sharp cleaver cut the lobster tail into slices. Cut the vermicelli into short lengths. Place vermicelli in a saucepan with dashi and bring to boil. Reduce heat and simmer for 5 minutes; add carrots, kombu and soy sauce. Simmer 2 minutes more. Add fish and lobster and simmer for 5 minutes or until ingredients are just cooked. Add mushrooms and spring onions during the last 1 or 2 minutes. Serve in soup bowls accompanied by small, individual dishes of dipping sauce. The ingredients are eaten with chopsticks and dipped in the sauce as desired. The soup is drunk from the bowl.

Dipping sauce: Put dashi, soy sauce and mirin in a small saucepan and bring to the boil. Remove from heat and cool. Add salt or sugar to taste.

steamed prawns

For simplicity it is hard to beat steamed prawns served with a dipping sauce. Remember the prawns must be fresh, not frozen.

serves 4

750 g (1½ lb) raw, medium-size prawns
salt
2 tablespoons light soy sauce
2 tablespoons dark soy sauce
2 teaspoons finely grated fresh ginger
2 teaspoons finely chopped spring onion
1 teaspoon finely chopped red chilli

Rub the prawns well with coarse salt. Rinse in a colander under cold water, then immerse prawns in a bowl of iced water for 10 to 15 minutes. Meanwhile combine sauces, divide in half and mix ginger and spring onion into one portion, the chilli into the other.

Bring a wok of water to the boil, place prawns in a steaming basket or wire strainer and steam over high heat for 7 or 8 minutes, just until prawns turn bright red. Put prawns on a serving plate and serve at once with the dipping sauces.

poultry

chicken and pineapple

serves 4

425 g (15 oz) can unsweetened
  pineapple pieces
375 g (12 oz) chicken breast fillets
  1 tablespoon cornflour
    salt to taste
    black pepper to taste
  1 tablespoon light soy sauce
  1 teaspoon oriental sesame oil
  ½ teaspoon crushed garlic
  1 teaspoon finely grated fresh
    ginger
  ½ tablespoon peanut oil
  4 spring onions, sliced on
    diagonal

Sauce
½ cup pineapple juice
2 teaspoons cornflour
1 tablespoon light soy sauce

Drain pineapple, reserving the juice for sauce. Cut chicken into thin slices, then toss in cornflour mixed with salt and pepper until well coated. Add soy sauce, sesame oil, garlic and ginger and mix with chicken.

In a wok, heat the peanut oil. Add the chicken and stir-fry just until colour changes. Add pineapple, lower heat, cover and simmer for 3 minutes.

Sauce: Gradually add the pineapple juice to the cornflour, mixing until smooth. Stir in soy sauce. Add this sauce mixture to the wok, stirring until it thickens. Toss in spring onions and mix through. Serve immediately with rice or noodles.

barbecued chicken kebabs

serves 4

750 g (1½ lb) boned and skinned chicken thighs
1 large onion, roughly chopped
2 cloves garlic, peeled
1 tablespoon finely chopped fresh ginger
juice of 2 limes or 1 lemon
1 teaspoon ground coriander
½ teaspoon ground cummin
1 teaspoon garam masala
⅓ cup plain low-fat yoghurt
1 teaspoon salt or to taste
2 tablespoons chopped fresh mint leaves

Remove any fat from the chicken thighs and cut into bite-size pieces. Place onion, garlic, and ginger in a food processor or blender and process until smooth, adding lime juice to facilitate mixing. Combine with ground spices, yoghurt, salt and mint leaves in a large bowl. Add the chicken pieces and stir to coat.

Marinate the chicken for 30 minutes at room temperature, or refrigerate overnight if possible. Thread chicken pieces on bamboo skewers and cook over glowing coals or under a preheated griller until cooked through. (Don't forget to soak bamboo skewers in water before use to prevent them burning.) Serve with rice or chapatis and onion, tomato and chilli salad (page 70).

chicken Himalaya

Serve this whole roast chicken warm or cold and accompanied by rice, Indian bread and/or salad.

serves 6

1.5 kg (3 lb) roasting chicken
1 teaspoon crushed garlic
1 teaspoon finely grated fresh ginger
1 tablespoon mild curry powder
1 teaspoon paprika
salt to taste
1 teaspoon garam masala (see page 91)
2 tablespoons lime or lemon juice
1 tablespoon soy sauce
1 tablespoon peanut or oriental sesame oil
2 tablespoons ground rice

Wash the chicken, removing excess fat, and dry well. Combine remaining ingredients to make a paste of spreading consistency. Rub over chicken inside and out and marinate for 1 hour. Roast in an oven preheated to 180°C (350°F) for 1¼ hours or until chicken is done. If surface browns too quickly during roasting, cover loosely with foil. Serve with rice or flat bread, and salad.

red cooked chicken

Simple simmering does not require any skill except to remember to keep the heat so low that the liquid does not bubble and boil. The more important part of this recipe is that stored heat is used to finish the cooking — once again that fuel-saving device so popular in the Chinese kitchen.

serves 4–6

1.5 kg (3 lb) chicken
1½ cups dark soy sauce
½ cup dry sherry
8 slices fresh ginger
2 cloves garlic
2 star anise
2 tablespoons sugar
2 teaspoons oriental sesame oil

Wash the chicken and dry with paper towels. Place in a saucepan into which it just fits, breast down. Mix together soy sauce, sherry, ginger, whole peeled garlic, star anise, sugar and 1 teaspoon sesame oil. Add 2 cups of water and pour the mixture over the chicken. Bring to the boil, then reduce heat, cover pan and simmer for 15 minutes.

Turn chicken over carefully, using tongs, cover and simmer for a further 20 minutes, basting chicken breast three times. Remove the pan from heat and leave covered until cool.

Place the chicken on a board and brush with remaining sesame oil. Cut into half lengthways, then turn cut side down on board and chop it into bite-size pieces through the bone. Arrange on a serving dish and serve with a little of the liquid.

Note: This may seem like an extravagant use of soy sauce, but remember that the cooking liquid becomes what is known as a Master Sauce. Cool and chill, remove and discard fat from surface. This sauce can be frozen and used over and over to simmer poultry and meats. To keep the sauce 'alive' it is necessary to use it from time to time.

roast spiced chicken

serves 6

3 spatchcocks, about 500 g (1 lb) each
¾ teaspoon saffron strands
6 cloves garlic, peeled, finely chopped
1½ teaspoons salt
1½ tablespoons finely grated fresh ginger
2 tablespoons lemon juice
1 teaspoon chilli powder
2 teaspoons garam masala
¾ cup low-fat natural yoghurt
½ tablespoon oil

Remove the skin from spatchcocks, slitting through skin front and back. Leave skin on wings (it is too difficult to try and remove it from these joints). Make slits in the flesh of the thighs, drumsticks and breast to allow spices to penetrate.

Toast saffron in a dry pan over gentle heat for a few seconds until dry and crisp, taking care strands do not burn. Turn the saffron onto a saucer and, when cool, crush with back of a spoon and dissolve in 2 tablespoons of hot water. Combine with garlic, salt, ginger and lemon juice, chilli powder, garam masala and yoghurt.

Rub spice mixture over the spatchcocks, especially in slits made in flesh. Cover and leave to marinate for at least 2 hours, or refrigerate overnight.

The best way to cook the birds is over a barbecue, first letting the fire burn down to glowing coals. Cut spatchcocks in halves lengthways, place on a rack and cook until tender, turning with tongs.

If this is not possible, preheat oven to 200°C (400°F). Place the spatchcocks, breast side down, in a roasting pan lined with lightly oiled foil or non-stick baking paper. Make sure the birds are not touching. Brush backs lightly with oil. Roast in a hot oven for 20 minutes, turn them over and continue roasting for a further 25 minutes or until done. If flesh appears to be drying out, cover pan loosely with foil. Serve hot, with flat bread and onion, tomato and chilli salad (page 70).

Kashmiri saffron chicken

serves 6

½ tablespoon oil
1 large onion, finely chopped
4 cloves garlic, finely chopped
2 teaspoons finely grated fresh ginger
3 fresh red chillies, seeded and sliced
½ teaspoon saffron strands
¼ teaspoon ground cardamom
1.5 kg (3 lb) prepared chicken pieces — breast, thighs and drumsticks — skin removed
salt to taste

Heat oil in a heavy frying pan and gently fry the onion, garlic, ginger and chillies, stirring frequently, until the onion is soft and golden. Heat the saffron in a dry pan over a low heat — do not let it burn. Crush and dissolve in 2 tablespoons very hot water. Add to frying pan with cardamom and stir well. Add the chicken and increase heat, turning the chicken to coat with saffron mixture. Add salt to taste, cover and cook over a moderate heat until the chicken is tender. Uncover and cook until liquid is reduced.

marinated grilled chicken

serves 6

750 g (1½ lb) chicken thigh fillets
6 tablespoons teriyaki barbecue sauce
6 spring onions

Trim all visible fat from the chicken and cut into bite-size pieces of equal size. Marinate for 1 hour in teriyaki sauce, or in a mixture of 4 tablespoons Japanese soy sauce, 2 teaspoons sake and 2 teaspoons sugar.

Cut the spring onions into short lengths and thread pieces of chicken and onion onto skewers. Cook over glowing coals or under a preheated griller until chicken is golden brown. Serve at once. Steamed rice may accompany chicken.

Note Soak bamboo skewers in cold water while preparing and marinating chicken to prevent them burning.

steamed egg roll

Most often served cold as part of a hors d'oeuvre selection, this tasty and nutritious combination of chicken and eggs is an ideal introduction to oriental flavours for youngsters. Serve with rice and lightly cooked green vegetables for a complete meal.

serves 4

Filling
185 g (6 oz) raw lean chicken, roughly chopped
salt to taste
2 teaspoons light soy sauce
½ teaspoon oriental sesame oil
¼ teaspoon finely grated fresh ginger
½ teaspoon crushed garlic
1 teaspoon cornflour
2 tablespoons finely chopped spring onions

Wrappers
4 eggs
salt to taste
½ tablespoon peanut oil
1 teaspoon oriental sesame oil

Filling: In a food processor, combine the chopped chicken with salt, soy sauce, sesame oil, ginger and garlic and process in short bursts until smooth, stopping and mixing mixture with spatula as necessary. Add the cornflour and spring onions, and process again. (Alternatively, chop all ingredients together with sharp chopper until mixture forms paste.)

Wrappers: Beat eggs with salt. Reserve 1 tablespoon to seal egg rolls. Heat small omelette pan; oil with paper towel dipped in both oils mixed together. Use 2 or 3 tablespoons of egg to make a thin omelette, cooking on one side. Flip onto a board. Repeat with remaining mixture to make 4 or 5 omelettes.

Divide filling according to number of omelettes. Spread filling almost to edges of the cooked side of each omelette with oiled spatula. Roll up Swiss-roll style, seal with reserved beaten egg. Lightly grease a plate and arrange rolls on it in a single layer. Cover and steam over boiling water for 15 minutes. Allow to cool a little before cutting into diagonal slices. Serve hot or cold.

braised chicken with wood fungus

Dried wood fungus (also known as 'cloud ears') swells to many times its size when reconstituted in water. It imparts no flavour of its own, but is prized in Chinese dishes for its resilient, crunchy texture.

serves 4

1 kg (2 lb) chicken pieces
4 – 6 pieces wood fungus
1 piece tender fresh ginger
2 cloves garlic
  pinch salt
10 pieces Szechwan pepper
1 tablespoon peanut oil
4 tablespoons dry sherry
2 teaspoons honey
3 tablespoons light soy sauce
2 segments of star anise

With a sharp cleaver, cut the chicken into bite-size pieces. Soak the wood fungus in hot water for 10 minutes; drain and cut into small pieces. Scrape the brown skin off ginger; cut into very thin slices and then into fine shreds until you have a tablespoonful. Crush garlic with pinch of salt. Lightly toast Szechwan pepper in a dry pan, then crush with a mortar and pestle or handle of a cleaver.

Heat a wok or heavy pan, add oil and fry ginger and garlic over low heat just until pale golden. Add the chicken pieces, increase heat to medium and stir-fry until chicken changes colour. Add crushed pepper, sherry, honey, soy sauce and star anise. Cover and simmer over low heat for 25 minutes, adding wood fungus pieces 5 minutes before end of cooking time. Add a little hot water if necessary.

tangerine chicken

serves 6

1 × 1.8 kg (3½ lb) roasting
  chicken
1½ tablespoons light soy sauce
  salt to taste
1 teaspoon sugar
1½ tablespoons dry sherry
1 piece dried tangerine peel,
  about the size of a bay leaf
1 whole star anise
3 tablespoons brown sugar
  (see Note)
fresh coriander sprigs to garnish

Remove any fat from chicken cavity. Wash chicken and dry with paper towels. Mix soy sauce, salt, sugar and dry sherry in a wide dish. Rub mixture inside and outside chicken. Marinate for 20 minutes, turning chicken twice. Place in a steamer and steam for 25 minutes.

Crush tangerine peel and star anise with a mortar and pestle as finely as possible and mix with brown sugar. Take a large, heavy saucepan or flameproof casserole with a well-fitting lid, deep enough to hold whole chicken on a rack or trivet. Line base with heavy duty foil, bringing it a little way up the side of pan. Sprinkle tangerine mixture evenly over foil, then place a trivet or wire rack on top. Place chicken on rack. Cover pan tightly and put over medium heat. When smoke begins to escape under lid, turn heat very low and smoke chicken for 20 minutes, or until done.

You can serve this dish hot or at room temperature. Slice flesh off bones and arrange on a platter. Garnish with sprigs of coriander.

Note The brown sugar is used for the smoking process only and does not add kilojoules to the dish.

white cut chicken

Stored heat is used here, and the 'hot and cold treatment' results in very white and tender chicken.

serves 6–8

1 small roasting chicken or 2 whole chicken breasts
1 stalk celery
3 slices ginger
1 small onion
1 star anise

Sauce
1 tablespoon honey
2 tablespoons oyster sauce
1 tablespoon soy sauce
¼ cup finely chopped spring onion
2 teaspoons finely grated fresh ginger
3 tablespoons toasted sesame seeds

Place whole chicken or breasts into a pan with cold water to cover. Add roughly chopped celery and ginger, onion and star anise. Bring to the boil, reduce heat, cover pan and simmer for 10 minutes.

Remove pan from heat and leave chicken to steep in liquid in covered pan for 15 minutes, then lift out chicken and submerge in a bowl of water with ice cubes for about 15 minutes, or until cold. Drain, cover and refrigerate for 2 hours or overnight. Bone chicken, slice meat thinly and arrange on a serving dish.

Sauce: Mix together honey, oyster sauce and soy sauce. Spoon over chicken and sprinkle with spring onion and ginger mixed together, then with toasted sesame seeds.

Note: In this recipe, chicken is cooked in stored heat in liquid to cover. The liquid is a good stock and may be used to cook rice. For best results, heat ½ tablespoon each peanut oil and sesame oil and gently fry 2 teaspoons finely chopped garlic. Add 2 cups rice and fry, stirring with a metal spoon, for 2 minutes. Add 3 cups hot stock, bring to the boil, then turn heat very low, cover pan tightly and cook for 20 minutes. Uncover and allow steam to escape. Serve.

chicken omelette

serves 4

6 eggs
4 tablespoons water
salt to taste
2 teaspoons Japanese soy sauce
vegetable oil for frying

Filling
8 strips carrot and 8 green beans
strips of cooked chicken breast
4 teaspoons Japanese soy sauce
2 teaspoons mirin or dry sherry
2 teaspoons sugar
2 teaspoons finely grated ginger

Filling: Boil carrot strips and beans until just tender. Marinate chicken in remaining ingredients.

Omelette: Beat the eggs with a fork. Add water, salt and soy sauce. Heat a large, heavy frying pan and oil lightly. Pour in half the egg and cook until it is set on the bottom but still creamy on the top. Place strips of chicken, carrot and beans at one end. Roll the omelette firmly around the filling. Turn onto a warm plate. repeat with the rest of the egg and filling. Cut each omelette into slices and serve warm with steamed rice. Chicken omelette can also be served cold as an hors d'oeuvre.

grilled
pepper chicken

Robustly flavoured with garlic, pepper and coriander, it is not for the faint hearted. Works well on a barbecue.

serves 6–8

2 kg (4 lb) chicken breast or thigh fillets
2 teaspoons salt
1 tablespoon crushed garlic (8–10 cloves)
3 tablespoons black peppercorns, coarsely crushed
6 fresh coriander plants, including roots, finely chopped
¼ cup lemon juice

Wash and dry chicken fillets, trimming off any visible fat. Lightly score the surface. Crush garlic with salt and mix with pepper, lemon juice and coriander. Rub over chicken and allow to stand for a couple of hours before cooking, or cover well and refrigerate overnight.

Cook chicken on a barbecue over glowing coals or under a preheated grill for about 5 minutes each side, or until well browned. Garnish with tomato wedges and cucumber slices. Serve with boiled rice or a crisp green salad.

stuffed chicken rolls

serves 4

3 chicken breast fillets
1 clove garlic
½ teaspoon salt
½ teaspoon finely grated ginger
¼ teaspoon five spice powder
1 tablespoon cornflour
1 tablespoon egg white
2 spring onions
   strips of red capsicum
   tender green beans or strips of
   zucchini

Flatten chicken fillets slightly with meat mallet or base of heavy bottle until an even thickness all over. Crush garlic with salt, combine with ginger, five spice powder, cornflour and egg white and spread on each side of chicken. Place spring onion and strips of vegetables on each fillet and roll chicken firmly to enclose. Brush rolls with soy sauce, or pour soy into a flat dish and turn rolls in soy a few times over 30 minutes.

Wrap each roll firmly in microwave proof plastic. Cook in microwave oven on full power for 10 minutes, allow to stand for 5 minutes. When cool, remove plastic and slice into rings to serve.

salads

rose petal salad

For this unusual Thai salad try to use old-fashioned roses which have a lovely fragrance. Whether from your garden or a shop, make sure they have not been sprayed with pesticides. Vary the meats and seafood in this salad according to your own taste. You will find crisp, fried garlic and shallots in Asian food stores.

serves 4

4 full-blown roses
2 cooked chicken breast fillets
1 cup small cooked prawns
1 cup shredded cooked pork
12 pink grapefruit segments
4 tablespoons crushed roasted
  peanuts
2 teaspoons crisply fried garlic

4 teaspoons crisply fried shallots
  few leaves of frilled lettuce
  cucumber slices
2 tablespoons fish sauce
2 teaspoons sugar
4 teaspoons lime juice
1 fresh red chilli, seeded and
  finely sliced

Carefully wash roses with cold water; shake gently and place on paper towels to drain, petals downwards. Cut chicken meat into thin strips; shell and devein prawns.

In a bowl mix chicken, prawns, pork, grapefruit segments, 2 tablespoons of peanuts, fried garlic and shallots. Arrange over lettuce leaves on individual plates. Garnish with cucumber slices.

In a small bowl stir fish sauce, sugar, lime juice and chilli until sugar dissolves. Spoon mixture over combined ingredients. Remove petals from roses and scatter over the top. Sprinkle with remaining peanuts

seafood salad

To prevent seafood becoming tough and rubbery, it is imperative to avoid overcooking.

serves 6

375 g (12 oz) raw prawns
375 g (12 oz) cleaned squid
3 kaffir lime leaves, fresh or dried
3 sprigs fresh coriander
1 stalk lemon grass, finely sliced
1 tablespoon fish sauce
3 tablespoons lime juice
1 teaspoon dark brown sugar
2 cloves garlic, crushed

2 teaspoons finely chopped ginger
freshly ground black pepper
$\frac{3}{4}$ cup finely sliced spring onions, including some green tops
$\frac{1}{3}$ cup lightly packed mint leaves
2 or 3 fresh red chillies, finely sliced

Shell and devein prawns (leaving tails on if desired). Slit and rinse squid tubes.

Wipe clean with kitchen paper if needed. With a sharp knife, score inside surface diagonally with narrow parallel lines, holding the knife at an angle of 45° to make cuts without going through. Cut scored squid into bite-size pieces.

Boil 3 cups of water in a small saucepan with lime leaves, coriander and lemon grass for 5 minutes. Drop in squid and immediately the pieces curl and turn opaque, remove with a slotted spoon. This should take less than 1 minute. Bring liquid back to boil and cook prawns, only until they turn pink. Lift out immediately with slotted spoon.

In a serving bowl, mix fish sauce, lime juice, sugar, garlic, ginger and pepper. Toss seafood in dressing, then add spring onions, mint and chillies and toss lightly.

onion, tomato and chilli salad

A typical salad served throughout India as an accompaniment to rice, curries and other main dishes.

serves 6

2 medium onions
salt
walnut-sized piece of dried
  tamarind pulp
2 tablespoons brown sugar
2 firm, ripe tomatoes
2 fresh red or green chillies, sliced
1 tablespoon finely shredded
  fresh ginger
2 tablespoons chopped coriander
  leaves

Cut onions in halves lengthwise and then across into fine slices. Sprinkle with plenty of salt and set aside for 1 hour. Press out all liquid, rinse with cold water and drain well.

Soak tamarind in ½ cup hot water until softened, squeeze to dissolve pulp and strain seeds and fibres. Add brown sugar to tamarind liquid and stir until dissolved.

Scald tomatoes, peel and dice. Mix all ingredients, add salt if necessary, cover and chill until ready to serve.

Thai chicken, prawn and fruit salad

A sour and salty, slightly hot dressing accentuates some very different flavours in the fruit. Vary the fruit according to what is in season.

serves 6

1 mango, peeled and sliced
1 orange, peeled and segmented
1 pink or white grapefruit, peeled and segmented
washed and dried lettuce leaves
half a ripe pineapple
1 × 185 g (6 oz) can water chestnuts, sliced finely
6 miniature tomatoes, washed and chilled
1 cup small seedless grapes, washed and chilled
2 chicken breast fillets, poached and sliced

375 g (12 oz) cooked prawns, shelled and deveined
2 tablespoons roasted salted peanuts, crushed

Dressing
1 tablespoon sugar
2 tablespoons fish sauce
2 tablespoons lime juice
2 red chillies, seeded and sliced
2 small cloves garlic, crushed to a smooth paste with 1 teaspoon of the sugar

Arrange mango, orange and grapefruit on lettuce leaves. Peel pineapple with a sharp stainless steel knife. Quarter lengthwise, discard core, then cut in thin slices. Arrange on a platter. Combine water chestnuts, tomatoes and grapes with chicken and prawns in a bowl. Sprinkle 2 tablespoons of dressing over, tossing to distribute flavours. Mound chicken and prawn mixture on platter beside arranged fruits. Place remaining dressing in a small serving bowl on platter with fruit for spooning over individual servings. Sprinkle crushed peanuts over salad just before serving.

Dressing: Dissolve sugar in ¼ cup cold water, then stir in remaining ingredients.

beef salad

serves 4

500 g (1 lb) rump, fillet or sirloin
steak
1 teaspoon chopped garlic
1 tablespoon chopped coriander
roots and stalks
1 teaspoon green peppercorns in
brine, drained
2 teaspoons raw sugar or
palm sugar
2 teaspoons Maggi Seasoning

1 tablespoon lime juice
2 teaspoons fish sauce
2 small seedless cucumbers
8 small purple shallots or 2 small
purple onions, sliced thinly
3 red chillies, seeded and sliced
1 stem lemon grass (tender white
part only) sliced thinly
fresh mint sprigs

Trim fat from steak. Barbecue over coals for best flavour, otherwise grill under preheated griller until medium rare. Cool until firm, then cut into thin slices.

Pound or crush garlic with coriander, peppercorns and sugar. Add Maggi Seasoning, lime juice and fish sauce; stir until smooth. Peel cucumbers, score with a fork and slice finely. Lightly toss all ingredients except mint. Serve in a salad bowl garnished with fresh mint.

lemon chicken salad

serves 4

750 g (1½ lb) chicken breast fillets
few celery leaves
1 large onion, halved
3 tablespoons Chinese bottled lemon sauce
1½ tablespoons dark soy sauce
⅓ cup finely chopped fresh coriander leaves and stems
1½ teaspoons finely grated fresh ginger
half a Chinese cabbage

Place chicken fillets in a saucepan with water to cover. Add celery leaves and onion and slowly bring just to simmering point. Cover and poach over very gentle heat for 6–8 minutes. Turn off the heat and allow the chicken to cool in the liquid. (Strain the liquid. Reserve this stock for future use.) Slice meat thinly and arrange on a platter.

Combine lemon sauce and soy sauce in a small bowl. Pour over chicken and leave to marinate for at least 30 minutes. Arrange on a serving dish and serve sprinkled with a mixture of chopped coriander and grated ginger on a bed of shredded Chinese cabbage.

meat

beef
in black bean sauce

Another dish to practise your stir-frying with. Notice how few ingredients there are, yet they give superb flavour and make meat go much further. From start to finish, it should not take more than 4 minutes to cook, if all ingredients are placed in readiness.

serves 4–6

500 g (1 lb) rump or fillet steak
2 tablespoons canned salted
black beans
2 cloves garlic, finely chopped
1 tablespoon dark soy sauce
1 teaspoon sugar
1 teaspoon cornflour
1 tablespoon peanut oil
125 g (4 oz) snow peas, blanched
½ teaspoon oriental sesame oil

Trim meat of all fat and freeze until just firm. Cut into paper-thin slices with a very sharp knife. Rinse black beans under cold water, drain, mash with a fork and combine with garlic. Mix soy sauce, sugar, cornflour and ¼ cup water.

Heat wok, add peanut oil and swirl to coat wok. Stir-fry beef over high heat until colour changes, then add beans and garlic. Stir-fry for a further 2 minutes. Add soy mixture, bring to the boil and stir constantly until thick. Sprinkle with sesame oil, add snow peas and mix well. Serve with steamed rice.

simmered
steak and vegetables

Paper-thin slices of meat and vegetables are dipped with chopsticks first into a boiling stock, and then into a Sesame Seed Sauce. The dish is eaten with rice and once all the steak and vegetables are consumed the stock is served as a soup. This is not taken with a spoon but drunk direct from bowls.

serves 6–8

1 kg (2 lb) fillet or rump steak, in one piece
1 small white Chinese cabbage
2 leeks
2 carrots
375 g (12 oz) button mushrooms
1 block tofu
8 to 10 cups chicken stock (see page 91)

Sesame seed sauce
⅓ cup sesame seeds
2 tablespoons rice vinegar or white wine vinegar
¾ cup Japanese soy sauce
3 tablespoons finely chopped spring onion
1 teaspoon finely grated fresh ginger
1 teaspoon sugar

Cut steak into very thin slices. (This is easier if meat is partially frozen.) Cut cabbage into short lengths. Wash leeks thoroughly to remove any grit and slice diagonally into bite-size pieces. Peel carrots and cut across in diagonal slices. Trim ends from mushrooms and wipe caps with paper towel. Cut tofu into squares. Arrange prepared food on a serving platter; cover and refrigerate until ready to serve.

If you have a shabu-shabu cooker or similar, pour stock into it. Alternatively use a table-top cooker or electric pan. Heat stock and place cooker in centre of table. Keep stock simmering throughout meal and add more if necessary.

Place a bowl, chopsticks and sauce dish at each setting. Set a large bowl of hot white rice on the table so that guests can serve themselves. Ingredients are picked from the serving platter with chopsticks and held in the boiling stock until just done, then transferred to individual bowls. Make sure that steak and vegetables are not overcooked. The meat should be pale pink and the vegetables tender but still crisp.

Sesame seed sauce: Toast sesame seeds in a small dry pan over moderate heat, stirring constantly, for about 5 minutes. Turn onto a plate to cool and then crush with a mortar and pestle. Mix with remaining ingredients, stirring until sugar dissolves. (The sauce can also be combined in a blender.)

sukiyaki

If you have the appropriate gas cooker or electric frying pan, you can cook this traditional one-pot meal at the table. Accompany it with bowls of hot white rice. It is customary for each diner to break an egg in a bowl, beat it lightly with chopsticks and then dip the freshly cooked hot food into it before eating.

serves 6

1 kg (2 lb) fillet, scotch fillet or
    rump steak in one piece
6 dried shiitake mushrooms
12 spring onions
1 small can winter bamboo
    shoots
2 tender carrots
2 medium onions
250 g (8 oz) fresh bean sprouts

1 small white Chinese cabbage
60 g (2 oz) bean thread vermicelli
6 pieces tofu (bean curd)
    vegetable oil
    Japanese soy sauce
    sugar
    sake or dry sherry
    beef stock
6 eggs, optional

Freeze steak for about an hour or until just firm enough to cut into very thin slices. Soak mushrooms in hot water for 30 minutes. Wash and trim spring onions and slice into bite-size pieces, including green portion. Drain bamboo shoots and slice thinly. Peel carrots and cut into julienne strips. Peel onions and cut lengthwise into eighths. Wash bean sprouts and remove any straggly tails. Wash cabbage and cut into bite-size pieces, discarding any tough leaves. Cook noodles in boiling water for 10 minutes, then drain and cut into short lengths.

Squeeze water from soaked mushrooms, discard stems and cut caps into slices. Arrange ingredients on a platter.

Heat a heavy frying pan with enough oil to film base of pan. Add half of each vegetable to pan and fry over high heat for 1 to 2 minutes, or until tender but still crisp. Push to one side of pan and add slices of meat in one layer. When cooked on one side, turn to cook the other (it will not take long since the meat is so thin). Sprinkle meat and vegetables with soy sauce, sugar and sake to taste, adding a little stock to moisten. Mix in noodles and tofu; heat through. Serve immediately—guests help themselves from the pan.

After the first batch has been consumed, more ingredients are added to the pan and cooked. Add more stock, soy sauce, sake and sugar and simmer as required.

steamboat dinner

The meats, seafood and vegetables of this dish are cooked in a full-flavoured boiling stock by guests at the table. If you don't have a 'steamboat' or 'firepot', you can use an electric wok. Accompany the dish with hot white rice and dipping sauces. Unless you have two cooking utensils, don't attempt serving this to more than 6 people.

serves 6

10 cups chicken stock (see page 91)	125 g (4 oz) snow peas or sugar snap peas
500 g (1 lb) fillet or rump steak	4 squares fresh bean curd
500 g (1 lb) chicken breast fillets or lean pork fillet	375 g (12 oz) Chinese vegetables
500 g (1 lb) raw prawns	250 g (8 oz) fresh bean sprouts
250 g (8 oz) fresh scallops	ginger-soy sauce (see below)
	chilli sauce (see below)

Partially freeze meats and cut into paper-thin slices. Shell and devein prawns. Wash and clean scallops if necessary. Remove strings from snow peas. Cut bean curd into thin slices. Trim any tough pieces from broccoli sprigs. Wash bean sprouts and pinch off straggly ends. Arrange meats, seafood and vegetables on separate serving platters.

In front of each diner set out a plate, bowl, porcelain spoon, chopsticks and individual sauce dishes. Fill steamboat or other cooking container three-quarters full with hot stock. Cover and place it in centre of table; allow stock to come to boil. Place a large bowl of hot white rice on table for guests to help themselves. Guests first select meat and seafood items of choice with chopsticks and hold them in the bubbling stock for no longer than 90 seconds. It is best to cook one type of food at a time as some take longer than others — do not overcook. These items are then dipped in sauce of choice. When meats and seafood have been consumed, add vegetables and bean curd to broth. Cover and simmer for a few minutes, then ladle soup into individual bowls.

Ginger-soy sauce: Combine 2 teaspoons finely grated fresh ginger, ¼ cup Japanese soy sauce, 2 tablespoons each sherry and water, 2 teaspoons sugar and 1 teaspoon sesame oil.

Chilli sauce: Choose a sweet or medium hot bottled chilli sauce. Put a little of each sauce into individual sauce dishes.

Note: Special wire spoons as shown in photograph may also be used for immersing food in the stock. These are available quite cheaply in Chinese stores.

fiery beef

serves 6

1 kg (2 lb) lean rump or fillet
   steak, in one piece
¼ cup soy sauce
2 tablespoons finely chopped
   spring onions
1 teaspoon crushed garlic
½ teaspoon finely grated fresh
   ginger
2 teaspoons sugar
¼ teaspoon black pepper
1 tablespoon toasted, crushed
   sesame seeds

Sauce
1 small clove garlic
   salt to taste
2 teaspoons sugar
3 tablespoons soy sauce
1 teaspoon sesame oil
2 tablespoons rice wine or dry
   sherry
1 teaspoon toasted, ground
   sesame seeds
2 teaspoons finely chopped spring
   onions
1 teaspoon chilli sauce

Partially freeze steak until firm—this will make it easier to slice. Cut steak into paper thin slices and then into bite-sized pieces. Mix remaining ingredients together with ¼ cup water in a large bowl. Add steak and leave to marinate, covered, for 3 hours or longer in refrigerator.

When ready to serve, grill steak briefly on an oiled grid placed over glowing coals on a barbecue. Serve accompanied by Sauce in small individual sauce bowls.

Sauce: Crush garlic to a fine paste with salt and sugar. Place in a small bowl and add remaining ingredients. Add 2 tablespoons water and stir together, mixing well.

Kashmiri roast lamb

This recipe will win fans with its gentle spicing and honeyed sweetness. Leftovers will star in salads or sandwiches.

serves 8

2 –2.5 kg (4–5 lb) leg of lamb
2 teaspoons finely grated fresh
   ginger
2 cloves garlic, crushed
   salt to taste
1 teaspoon ground cummin
1 teaspoon ground turmeric
1½ teaspoons garam masala (see
   page 91)

½ teaspoon saffron strands
1 cup natural yoghurt
2 tablespoons ground almonds
1 tablespoon honey
2 tablespoons blanched
   pistachios, optional

Remove skin and excess fat from lamb. With tip of knife, make deep slits in lamb.

Mix together ginger, garlic, salt and spices, adding a little oil to facilitate spreading if mixture appears too dry. Rub over lamb and into each slit.

Toast saffron strands in dry pan over low heat for 1 or 2 minutes, turn onto saucer

and when cool and crisp, crush with back of a spoon. Dissolve in 2 tablespoons boiling water. Combine with yoghurt, almonds and honey. Place lamb in large baking dish and spoon yoghurt purée over. Cover and place in refrigerator. Marinate lamb for 2 days if possible, or at least overnight.

Preheat oven to very hot, 230°C (450°F), and roast lamb in covered baking dish for

30 minutes. Lower heat to moderate, 180°C (350°F), and cook for further 2 hours or until lamb is cooked through. Uncover and leave lamb to cool to room temperature. Slice and serve with pocket bread and salad, or with steamed long grain rice.

beef
pot roast

A favourite in the Philippines but usually much richer because the beef is larded with pork fat. This recipe keeps the flavour but drops the fat.

serves 6

1.5 kg (3 lb) blade steak in one piece
3 large onions, quartered
3 large tomatoes, halved
1 bay leaf
½ cup vinegar

3 cloves garlic, chopped
1 tablespoon finely chopped fresh ginger
2 tablespoons light soy sauce
6 potatoes, peeled and halved
freshly ground black pepper

Trim any fat from beef and discard. Put meat into a deep, heavy saucepan or flameproof casserole just slightly larger than the beef. Surround with onions, tomatoes, bay leaf, vinegar, garlic, ginger and soy sauce. Bring to boil, then reduce heat, cover pan and simmer until meat is almost tender (about 1½ hours).

Add potatoes and plenty of freshly ground pepper and simmer until potatoes are cooked. Baste meat from time to time. When cooked, slice meat and arrange on serving platter, adding sauce and potatoes.

beef
and vegetable stew

Serve this stew with white rice and small bowls of extra fish sauce, soy sauce, a hot chilli sauce or a traditional Filipino mixture of equal quantities of bottled shrimp sauce and lime juice.

serves 6

1 oxtail, jointed
750 g (1½ lb) shin beef on bone, sliced
3 teaspoons salt, or to taste
2 tablespoons vegetable oil
2 teaspoons annatto seeds
2 large onions, sliced very finely
8 large cloves garlic, finely chopped
1 teaspoon ground black pepper
3 tablespoons roasted rice powder

½ cup roasted peanuts, crushed or pounded
250 g (8 oz) tender green beans, cut in halves
4 slender eggplants, halved lengthways
2 tablespoons fish sauce, or to taste
2 tablespoons sliced spring onion, including green parts
2 tablespoons chopped celery leaves

Put oxtail and shin of beef into a large pan with water to cover and salt to taste. Bring to boil and simmer until almost tender, about 2 hours. Cool to lukewarm and strain. Chill stock and remove fat from surface. (Use a pressure cooker if you have one: put oxtail and shin into cooker with just enough water to cover and salt to taste. Cook under pressure for 1 hour.)

Dry pieces of partially cooked meats with paper towels. Heat 1 tablespoon oil in a large, deep saucepan or flameproof casserole and brown pieces, a few at a time, turning with tongs. Transfer each batch to a plate as it cooks. Pour off any fat from pan and heat remaining oil; fry annatto seeds on low heat for 1 minute, covering pan as they pop when they become hot. Remove pan from heat and lift out seeds on a slotted spoon. The oil will now have become a bright orange colour. Add onions and garlic and fry over medium heat, stirring frequently, until soft — about 10 minutes. Return meat to pan. Reheat stock, adding sufficient hot water to make 8 cups. Pour over meat, add pepper and bring to boil. Turn heat low and simmer, partially covered, until meat is tender.

Meanwhile combine roasted rice powder (sold in Asian stores) with peanuts. If rice powder is not readily available, make it at home—the flavour is essential in this dish. Put rice into a heavy frying pan and roast over medium heat, stirring frequently, and shaking pan so that grains colour evenly. When deep golden, allow to cool slightly, then grind to a powder in an electric blender.

Test meat which should be tender enough to easily pierce with a fork, but not falling off bone. Add more water to just cover meat if necessary. Add rice and peanut mixture, stirring until smooth. Stir beans and eggplant into stew and cook, uncovered, until vegetables are tender. Add fish sauce to taste. Serve hot, sprinkled with spring onion and celery leaves.

stir-fried chilli beef

serves 4–6

500 g (1 lb) lean fillet or rump steak, in one piece
1 tablespoon peanut oil
1 teaspoon finely chopped garlic
1 teaspoon finely chopped fresh ginger
¾ cup thinly sliced spring onions
1 teaspoon chilli sauce
90 g (3 oz) snow peas
½ cup thinly sliced celery
2 teaspoons cornflour
½ teaspoon sesame oil

Freeze steak until firm and then cut into paper-thin slices. Heat wok; add peanut oil and swirl to coat. Add garlic, ginger and half the spring onions. Stir-fry for 1 minute on low heat. Add meat and stir-fry on high heat, tossing meat so that all surfaces brown. Add chilli sauce, snow peas and celery and stir-fry for 30 seconds. Mix cornflour with ½ cup water and add to wok. Bring to boil, stirring, then add sesame oil and remaining spring onions. Mix and serve immediately.

glossary

Bean curd
Made from soy beans and high in protein. Available in various forms: soft, firm, fried or in tetra packs.

Besan
Chick pea flour, sold at Indian shops and many health food stores. It has a strong, distinctive flavour and the nearest substitute is pea flour, but this must be sifted through a very fine sieve as it is usually much coarser.

Chicken stock
2 kg (4 lb) chicken soup pieces, 3 litres (12 cups) cold water, 1 teaspoon of black peppercorns, 8 slices of fresh ginger, 3 stalks of celery with leaves, 2 onions peeled and halved, a few stalks of fresh coriander including roots, salt to taste.
Put chicken pieces in a large saucepan. Add remaining ingredients and bring to the boil. Cover and simmer for 1½ hours. Add salt to taste.
Use this stock as a starting point. To reduce the fat content, chill the stock until fat globules solidify on the surface, then lift off. Add noodles and this stock makes a quick and tasty meal for children. Or make egg drop simply by pouring beaten egg into the boiling stock.

Chillies
Fresh chillies should be handled with care as the volatile oils can cause much discomfort. Small chillies are hotter than large ones. Wear gloves when handling. It is possible to buy fresh chopped chillies in jars which may be substituted, and also Sambal Oelek (Ulek) which is a mixture of fresh chillies and salt. Or there is Tabasco Pepper Sauce. Use 1 teaspoon in place of each hot chilli.

Coriander
Coriander seeds and fresh coriander are different in flavour and usage. Dried ground coriander seeds are one of the main ingredients in curries; fresh coriander herb is an essential ingredient in Thai and Chinese cooking.

Cummin
Sold as whole seeds or ground, this spice has a lemony fragrance and is a major component of curries.

Garam masala
Essential in Indian dishes. Roast separately until fragrant—2 tablespoons coriander seeds, 1 tablespoon cummin seeds, 2 teaspoons whole black peppercorns, 1 teaspoon cardamom seeds (remove from pods), 2 cinnamon sticks and 10 whole cloves. Grind as finely as possible and mix in half a nutmeg, finely grated. Store airtight.

Ginger
Fresh rhizomes are usually available at any greengrocer. Dried ground ginger is no substitute in Asian cooking.

Maggi Seasoning
A flavouring that, the manufacturers claim, contains no added monosodium glutamate (MSG). It is given here as a substitute for Golden Mountain sauce, which is similar, but contains MSG.

Mirin
Japanese sweet rice wine, used only for cooking. Sweet sherry may be substituted, though flavour is not the same.

Nori
Laver seaweed, sold in thin sheets.

Saffron
Try to get true saffron because there are many imitations and nothing else has the same flavour. Expensive, but very little is needed and it keeps well if stored airtight. It is sold in strands (best to buy these) or tiny packets of powder. There is no such thing as cheap saffron.

Sesame oil
Use oriental sesame oil made from roasted sesame, which is darker in colour and very aromatic. Light coloured sesame oil (usually sold in health food stores) will not impart the same flavour.

Shiitake mushroom
Dried Chinese or Japanese mushrooms are the Shiitake variety. Dried European mushrooms are no substitute.

Star anise
A dried, star-shaped seed pod that imparts flavour to Chinese food. Simmered in long-cooked dishes.

Szechwan pepper
Small berries that are not hot in the conventional sense, but leave a numbing sensation on the tongue. Only the brown husks provide flavour, so buy the seeded variety. Roast over a low heat to bring out the aroma, and crush to powder.

Turmeric
A tropical rhizome, it is most readily available as a yellow powder used to flavour and colour food.

index